TRUTH BEYOND
RELATIVISM:
KARL MANNHEIM'S
SOCIOLOGY OF
KNOWLEDGE

The 1977 Pere Marquette
Theology Lecture

TRUTH BEYOND RELATIVISM: KARL MANNHEIM'S SOCIOLOGY OF KNOWLEDGE

By GREGORY BAUM

Professor of Theology and Religious Studies
St. Michael's College,
University of Toronto

Marquette University Press
Milwaukee, Wisconsin 53223
March 27, 1977

Library of Congress Catalog Number 77-76605

ISBN 0-87462-509-2

Preface

In conjunction with the Tercentenary Celebration of the missions and explorations of Jacques Marquette, S.J., the University's namesake, the Marquette University Theology Department in 1969 launched a series of annual public lectures by distinguished theologians under the title of "The Pere Marquette Theology Lectures."

The 1977 lecture was delivered at Marquette University on March 27, 1977, by Professor Gregory Baum, Professor of Theology and Religious Studies at St. Michael's College in the University of Toronto.

Professor Baum was born in 1923 in Berlin, Germany. As a young man he went first to England and then in 1940 to Canada. In his undergraduate work at McMaster University, Hamilton, Ontario, he majored in mathematics and physics. His Bachelor of Arts degree was awarded to him in 1946. A year later he took his Master of Arts degree in mathematics at

Ohio State University. The University of Fribourg in Switzerland awarded him the doctorate in theology in 1956. More recently (1969-71) he spent two years at the New School in New York City studying and researching in the field of sociology. Over the years he has been the recipient of honorary doctorates from five Canadian and American colleges and universities.

Widely known as an author and lecturer, Professor Baum has not only published numerous articles but has also been editor of *The Ecumenist* and on the editorial boards of the *Journal of Ecumenical Studies* and of *Concilium.* His major books include: *That They May Be One* (1958), *The Jews and the Gospel* (1961), *Progress and Perspective* (1962), *Ecumenical Theology Today* (1965), *The Credibility of the Church Today* (1968), *Faith and Doctrine* (1969), *Man Becoming* (1970), and *New Horizon* (1972). His latest book, *Religion and Alienation,* was published by the Paulist Press in 1975. Professor Baum was also a member of the Secretariat for

Christian Unity during the time of the Second Vatican Council.

The present lecture reflects Professor Baum's considerable interest in the sociology of knowledge and his belief that insights from this area can be applied with great benefit not only to theological method but also to ecclesiology.

TRUTH BEYOND RELATIVISM: KARL MANNHEIM'S SOCIOLOGY OF KNOWLEDGE

"From the beginning of its history, the church has learnt to express the message of Christ with the help of ideas and terminology of various peoples, and has tried to clarify it with the wisdom of philosophers. The church's purpose has been to adapt the Gospel to the grasp of ordinary people as well as to the needs of the learned insofar as appropriate. Indeed, this accommodation of the revealed Word ought to remain the law of all evangelization. Each nation then develops the ability to express Christ's message in its own way."[1]

In this famous passage, Vatican Council II acknowledges the historicity of Christian truth in the church and raises the difficult question of relativism. The same Gospel has been proclaimed in a variety of ways and the moral stances of Christians have changed from age to age. To illustrate the historicity of the church's public teaching, allow me to refer to three famous ecclesiastical documents. In the *Syllabus of Errors*, promulgated in the sixties of the last century, the European church repudiated the emerging liberal society and the civil liberties and democratic culture associated with it. In *Gaudium et Spes*, drawn up by Vatican Council II, the church, under the influence of bishops and theologians from the industrialized nations, affirmed the modern world in its development toward greater freedom, greater prosperity, greater technological achievements, and greater participation of people in the making of public policy. Three years later, in the *Medellin Document*, the Latin American bishops, looking at this North Atlantic development from the viewpoint of the underdeveloped nations, perceived the maximizing economic and cultural institutions of the West as sources of exploitation and dependency, and advocated both the liberation of the exploited and global, bold, urgent, and deeply renovating social

change. For better or for worse, there is
pluralism in Christianity. Since we live in
an age of transition, the older ones among
us even remember the time when we ourselves had a perception of the Gospel that
was significantly different from our present one, leading to different affirmations of
truth and different kinds of action. Beyond
this inner-Christian pluralism, Christian
thinkers who have engaged in dialogue
with followers of other religions and learnt
to recognize in these religions what Vatican II called "a ray of the divine light,"
have been bound to relativize the absolute
character of Christianity and create theological space for the other religions before
God. This pluralism within the Christian
tradition and within the religious history
of the world raises the difficult question as
to how we can still without inner contra-
diction affirm absolute truth, a truth that
transcends history and is the same yester-
day, today and forever.

Relativity and transcendence raise theological and philosophical problems. Many
years ago, Professor Emil Fackenheim gave

at Marquette a lecture dealing with historicity and metaphysics, in which he tried to show from a philosophical point of view how one can recognize the historical character of all truth and at the same time affirm truth that transcends history, valid for all ages and all social groups.[2] It may come as a surprise to some that relativity and transcendence is also an issue in sociology, especially in the sociology of knowledge, which affirms the historicity of all knowledge and at the same time, to protect its own sphere of competence, wants to defend the existence of universal norms. The lecture I propose to deliver, then, is an exercise in sociological thinking, focusing on Karl Mannheim's foundational work, *Ideology and Utopia*.[3] In my effort to systematize Mannheim's approach to relativity and transcendence I shall try to bring out the elements of his theory that may be useful to Christian theology even though I do not have the space to deal with the theological issues in a systematic way.

Let me begin this discussion with the essential insight of sociology, expressed in one way or another by all sociologists and most dramatically by Karl Marx, namely, that human consciousness is produced by the institutions, social, economic, and political, in which people live. Consciousness is from the beginning a social product. We produce the material conditions of our common existence which in turn constitute our mind-set and our style of thought. "Life is not determined by consciousness," writes Marx in his *German Ideology,* "but consciousness by life."[4] Neither Marx nor any of the classical sociologists understood this principle in a reductionist way as if socially determined consciousness left no room for personal freedom. They simply meant that the institutions men create for their common life and the pressures of history to which they are exposed produce in them a determinate consciousness, but they did not deny in any way that within this social determination room is left for

personal creativity and that at certain historical moments the original responses of
personal consciousness are able to affect
the social conditions of life and thus re-
direct the movement of history.

To persuade his readers that such a
determination of consciousness is not con-
trary to the intuition of freedom, Karl
Mannheim used to refer to the sphere of
the fine arts. Who could be freer than the
artist? Who is less determined by social
norms and mores than the painter? And
yet, when he paints a picture responding
to his creative genius alone, we recognize
the painting immediately as, say, fifteenth
century Florentine, and, if we are art historians, we can even decipher the decade
and the school to which it belongs. Here
we have, then, personal originality and yet
total social determination. Whether the
analogy from the sphere of art applies also
to reason and the realm of thought is
studied in the sociology of knowledge.

A first basic principle of Karl Mannheim's sociology of knowledge is that no
mode of thought can be understood unless

its social origin has been clarified. Ideas are generated as people struggle with the issues important in their society, and the meaning and import of these ideas cannot be properly understood unless one takes into account their social foundation. This does not mean, of course, that ideas can be judged as right or wrong simply by examining their social origins, but it does mean that ideas must be understood in relation to the people who produce them and hold them and in whose lives they play a role.

Theologians are familiar with this principle. For in biblical studies it has been taken for granted for a long time that a biblical passage or a biblical idea cannot be understood unless it be placed into its *Sitz im Leben*. The German phrase used in this context reminds us that this principle is drawn from German historiography, in fact from the historicist trend of German thought, whence is derived the sociology of knowledge itself. The meaning of a sentence cannot be understood unless we place it in the conversation in which it was uttered, and in turn a conversation cannot be understood unless we situate it in the actual historical conditions under which it was held. Theologians have come to take for granted that one cannot remove a sentence, however reliable, from ancient texts, be they even the Christian creeds, and then repeat it in a contemporary religious conversation and expect that it will retain its original meaning. To repeat what the ancient sentence said demands a hermeneutical exercise, in which its *Sitz im Leben* plays a significant role.

There is a trend in contemporary hermeneutics, derived from Paul Ricoeur and Hans-Georg Gadamer, to look upon a written text as an objectification of thought, having an existence in itself, that must be understood not by inquiring into its social origin, which is irrelevant, but by permitting oneself to be addressed, questioned, and confronted by the text, and thus to enter upon a journey of self-discovery.[5] By situating the text into its original historical context, it is argued, we distance ourselves from it, we escape its power, and we prevent ourselves from learning anything new from it. This appoach is largely derived from the study of art, and it is useful when applied to the interpretation of music, beautiful objects and symbolic gestures, where research into social foundations adds very little. But if this approach were applied to the study of texts that embody modes of thought and express ideas, it would certainly run counter to the insights of the sociology of knowledge. It is true, of course, that writing a text is an objectification of thought that gives it a certain independent existence apart from its author and his conditions. Still, the writing of the text is an historical act that fits into some concrete project of world building and cannot be understood adequately without taking this into consideration.

It can be argued that at the present time critical historical scholarship of the Bible has so swamped theological education and the entire theological enterprise that educated Christians have become estranged from the biblical message. They no longer dare to respond to the biblical text in faith, they no longer know how to surrender themselves to God's message in the text. Why? Because they have been made to feel that they must first consult a biblical commentary, grasp the conditions under which the text was written, and only then try to interpret its meaning for the present day. To make the Bible speak again, to permit Christians to surrender themselves again to the sacred book and to sacred symbols, the new hermeneutical approach may well be important and useful. There is something to be said for letting the Bible, in a direct and unmediated way, address us, convict us of sin and restore us to new life. But when this approach is generalized and established as the principal approach to hermeneutics, it offends against the more assured approach of the sociology of knowledge.

These few remarks on the new hermeneutics, I wish to add, have already been an exercise in the sociology of knowledge. Why? Because to understand this new mode of thought we took into account its social origin. We tried to understand the

aim and purpose of the new hermeneutics
in theology, not indeed to evaluate the
new method but to limit its scope and
highlight its power.

What is the social origin of the sociology
of knowledge? This surely is a question we
cannot avoid. It is not surprising that this
question is posed and answered at the beginning of Karl Mannheim's *Ideology and
Utopia*.[6] What were the historical conditions under which social thinkers devel-
oped the sociology of knowledge? If
knowledge is socially dependent—the Germans call it *standortgebunden*—the sociology of knowledge cannot be immune from
this. Karl Mannheim thought that the sociology of knowledge and the relativizing
of truth that accompanied it became pos-
sibilities only when through social up-
heavals people encountered several world
views in their own sphere of life, either because they themselves had moved through
a radical shift of perception or because
they were obliged to make joint decisions
with men who had lived far away but who
through this upheaval had come closer

and intermingled with them. These were the historical conditions of Germany after World War I. The conflict taking place between various groups in Germany was not just about ideas, whether they were true or false, but about world views, about the total perception of reality. To argue about the truth or falsehood of an idea makes sense only if the two partners share the same world view. If the two interlocuters belong to different and separate social worlds and operate out of different social perspectives, then such an argument is an exercise in futility and makes people talk past one another. The intentionality, then, behind the sociology of knowledge was to produce a consensus that made social life possible among people, groups and classes that have different historical backgrounds and different social locations and that consequently see the world in different perspectives. Max Scheler was the first social thinker to see this clearly, and Karl Mannheim, who followed upon Scheler, wholeheartedly agreed with him, even if he differed from Scheler on other issues. In

the early twenties, Scheler, seeing that the
world was becoming a global community,
demanded a new approach to truth, one
that could bring East and West in fruitful
conversation and engage them in a common project.[7] This new approach, Scheler
thought, was the sociology of knowledge.

Scheler and Mannheim admitted, of
course, that truth of the kind $2+2=4$ is
meaningful quite apart from its social
foundation and hence enjoys universal
validity, and they were quite willing to
extend this universality to the sphere of
the natural sciences, more readily, possibly,
than is done by some contemporary scientists. But what they both insisted on, even
though for very different reasons, was that
$2+2=4$ must not be made the model of
all knowledge. Scheler vehemently polemicized against the attempt of positivists to
make scientific knowledge normative truth.
In fact, the immediate and clearly stated
motive for creating his sociology of knowledge was his passionate desire to refute
the Comtean prejudice that religion and
philosophy would eventually give way to

science. Scheler tried to show that the de-
cline of religion and metaphysics and the
hegemony of scientific knowledge in modern society were associated with the rise of
the bourgeoisie, the class that defined itself in terms of economic interests.[8] Religion and metaphysical wisdom became
obsolete in a society that made people
define themselves in terms of expanding
production and the maximization of profit.

Mannheim was not a religious person;
he was wholly secular. But he too argued
against the attempt of the natural sciences
to make themselves the measure of
truth. Mannheim vehemently polemicized
against positivism. He argued that the
method of the natural sciences, including
mathematics, which plays such an essential part in it, cannot be extended to the
human sciences, the *Geisteswissenschaften*
as the Germans call them, i.e., the social
sciences and the study of history. Positivism is blind to the human reality and for
this reason has a devastating effect on
society.

One of his sets of arguments I wish

to present in greater detail. Following
the classical sociologists, especially Max
Weber, Mannheim insisted that human
action was constituted by two dimensions,
behaviour and meaning. To understand
social action, therefore, the social scientist
must study a) external behaviour, and here
the scientific method is indeed applicable,
and b) the meaning of this behaviour, and
here a hermeneutical approach is required.
Mannheim distinguished between three
different kinds of meaning which social
action may have—and I believe that this
classification is original with him—namely,
objective meaning, which is defined by the
social context in which the action takes
place, *expressive* meaning, which is attrib-
uted to the action by the actor, and,
thirdly, *documentary* meaning, often quite
hidden from the actor, which expresses an
aspect belonging to the culture as a whole.[9]
The objective meaning of football, to give
a simple example, is defined by the rules
of the game itself. The expressive meaning
assigned by a player to his action depends
on his personal history. He may engage in

football, for instance, to please his father or to win a scholarship. Is there also a third, more hidden meaning of football, in which the social scientist should be interested? Why is it, a social scientist must ask, that football is such a popular sport? Why does it draw people's attention? Why do they spend so much money watching it at the stadium and so much time looking at one game after another on the television screen? Why this social addiction to football? Football has power over the minds of men in our society because something of this society expresses itself in the game. Something hidden in the culture, operating in people's lives in an unconscious or unthematized fashion, finds expression in football: this is documentary meaning. If social scientists want to deal with this, the most significant meaning of social action, then they must look at society as a whole and engage in a process of observation, interpretation and evaluation through which they can grasp the concrete form of social life in its totality and discover how this expresses itself in particular actions. Posi-

tivism has no access to documentary meaning: it makes people blind to the human
reality. What sociologists seeking documentary meaning cannot avoid—and this
is a point dear to critical sociologists—is to
apply some norms in their account of the
social process and to discern in society the
conflict between human values and their
destruction. But how can they do this? Are
there norms that transcend their own social
heritage? We have returned to the topic
of this lecture.

We conclude from the above remarks
that to argue against the sociology of
knowledge by insisting that $2+2=4$ is universally true is based on the inadequate
presupposition that mathematics and the
natural sciences connected with it constitute the privileged model of truth.

We now mention a second principle of
the sociology of knowledge, related to the
first, which will be important to us later
in this lecture. Ideas and modes of thought,
related as they are to social entities, change
in meaning as these social bodies—Mannheim calls them "carriers" (*Träger*)—under-

go significant historical change. As these
bodies shift their historical location a shift
also takes place in the meaning or the style
of thought associated with them. A single
sentence may change its meaning when its
social "carrier" moves to a different position
of power. The development of ideas takes
place less through intrinsic derivations by
means of logic than through the concrete
historical changes in the social "carrier"
and the need to rethink the inherited ideas
from the new location.

An ironic example of this principle is the
changed meaning of the German anthem,
"Deutschland, Deutschland über alles." In
the first half of the 19th century, this was
a revolutionary song expressing the ardent
desire for national unity and freedom from
the domination of the princes. Germany
"über alles" then meant "above all" the di-
visions created by the feudal order. After
the unification of Germany under the
ambitious Prussian crown, the same song
acquired a new meaning. It now expressed
an aggressive stance toward other nations,
Germany "above all" the others in the

world. Any revolutionary ideology promoted by a minority struggling for its
place under the sun acquires a new meaning after the success of the revolution and
the shift in power relations. Unless this is
clearly recognized, the old radical ideology
becomes a set of ideas legitimating the new
order of things and thus preparing new
patterns of domination. The Daughters of
the American Revolution do not stand for
the upheaval of the political order but for
its defense.

This principle applies to all forms of
thought, not only to revolutionary ideas.
Mannheim himself used this principle to
distinguish between traditionalism and
conservatism. Traditionalism is the taken-
for-granted acceptance of the inherited
world view. Yet once the dominant culture
of the inherited society has been chal-
lenged and a new class emerges in society
and reaches for power, a change takes
place in the social base of the inherited
world view. The social base becomes one
interest group in society surrounded by
others; and when this group affirms and

defends the traditional world view, then
this is no longer done spontaneously but
with deliberation, as a reply to the chal-
lenge, with new sets of arguments. What
is being defended now is a whole style of
life and a social order in which this group
exercises unquestioned power. The traditional world view, in Mannheim's terminology, becomes conservative thought.
Thus Scholasticism in the middle ages was
a cultural achievement universally respected. When it was revived in the 19th
century under the auspices of the papacy—
I refer here to a monograph on the sociology of knowledge background of the
Thomistic revival[10]—its meaning changed
significantly. It was now a system of
thought that defined itself over against
various other philosophies and took part in
a conflict between several groups seeking
hegemony in Europe. It became above all
a philosophy that promoted the power of
the ecclesiastical institution and the social
orders which respected and defended this
power.

According to Karl Mannheim, the history of ideas should not be studied as if the development of thought takes place primarily in the minds of the thinkers—to do this would disguise the social foundation of thought—but as a wider historical investigation that relates the ideas to their social base, examines the changes in the location of the social base, and only then analyses the ideas that emerge in the new setting.[11] If this principle is correct, then the development of doctrine in the church cannot be adequately studied unless the individual doctrines are related to the concrete historical circumstances in which they were formulated. This method may restrict the universal application of doctrinal formulations, but it brings out the salvational meaning of doctrines and hence enables the theologian to express their evangelical content in contemporary terms.

The sociology of knowledge, defined by the two principles mentioned above, leads to a certain relativizing of truth. Truth, values, norms of any kind are situated in a particular community and correspond to concrete historical circumstances. There seems to be no good reason to attribute to them universal validity. The sociology of knowledge agrees with the Marxian position that the ideas that lay claim to universality are the ideas of the dominant class or its culture, which understands itself as the norm of humanity and thus promotes and legitimates its superior power. In this perspective the idea of human nature appears as the self-understanding of the successful class elevated as the norm to which other people must conform. But is it possible, beyond this relativity of truth, to affirm universal values and a truth that transcends history?

Let me explain first that the founders of the sociology of knowledge, Max Scheler and Karl Mannheim, vehemently opposed the two kinds of relativism they encountered in their own culture. They hoped that their sociological approach would enable the social thinker to move beyond relativism, which in their eyes constituted an enormous social danger. What were these two forms of relativism?

There was, first of all, the relativism of

positivistically oriented social scientists
who considered their own research value-
neutral and who saw the norms affirmed
by people in various cultures as so many
basically arbitrary ways in which they defined themselves to assure their survival
and well-being. This objectivist stance,
along with ethical relativism, still domi-
nates many university departments in our
own day. As I mentioned above, Scheler
and Mannheim polemicized against positivism. They opposed the idea of a value-
free social science. They insisted that the
mind, even the logical mind of scientists,
is historically constituted and hence reflects the culture to which they belong and
the social perspective they have either
consciously or unconsciously adopted. Social scientists look upon the human reality,
whether past or present, from a particular
point of view. There is no place outside of
history from which social thinkers can examine society. Of course, social scientists
must try to overcome their prejudices, re-
fine their readings, perfect their logic,
broaden their base, submit their rational

arguments to criticism, and test in conversation with their colleagues the validity of
their insights—and in this sense try to be
as "objective" as possible; but they must at
the same time clarify their underlying pre-
suppositions, understand their own location in society, and render a critical account of their social ideals. There is no
presuppositionless research. Truth remains
standortgebunden, socially dependent,
even in the human sciences.

We note that in speaking of the social
dependence of sociological research we
are not simply referring to distortions of
scientific conclusions due to the social limitations of the researcher. Even positivists
agree that the objectivity they praise is an
ideal and that in fact a certain bias in
sociological studies is almost inevitable.
According to the sociology of knowledge,
however, the historical location of the researcher is not only a source of error; it
also provides a special perspective from
which an aspect of truth becomes visible
that is not otherwise available. The truth
about the human reality cannot be dis-

covered by one tradition of thought alone nor from a single cultural perspective. Each culture, and in fact each important school of thought within each culture, lays hold of an aspect that may be neglected by others. Mannheim even spells out the positive contribution of positivism by locating it in its original struggle against obscurantism, superstition, and the mystification of the truth on the part of church and state for the sake of their institutional interests. The truth about the human reality, moreover, cannot be discovered equally from all locations within the same culture or the same society, by oppressor and oppressed alike. While Mannheim denounces the ideological deformations operative in the perspective of the oppressor and attributes great importance to the neglected perspective of the oppressed, he admits that the exploited struggling for emancipation also tend to distort their vision. Even radical movements should recognize that their ideas are partial and in need of balance and complement from other perspectives. These things are said, as we shall see later, not to propose an easy formula of reconciliation but to gain a correct understanding of true differences.

Scheler and Mannheim extended their argumentation against positivistic science and the ethical relativism associated with it. For Scheler, natural science was instrumental knowledge oriented toward the control of nature and the development of a technological society. In the natural sciences, Scheler thought, the observer regards himself superior to the object he studies; he rules over it, he disposes of it, he picks it up and then drops it again. Exclusive dedication to science leads to a mind-set of domination, creates a society based on power, and makes people appear as objects to be known and manipulated. Positivism is the expression of the bourgeoisie: it is the appropriate intellectual outlook of a class that stands for the domination of nature and the subjugation of the masses as wage labourers.

Mannheim polemicized against positivism in his own way. He too regarded as dangerous the application of the scien-

tific method to the human sciences. Positivism quantifies and reifies human life and
devours living human beings. Mannheim
also understood the quantification of
thought through positivism as a reflection
in the sphere of the mind of the quantification of life through capitalist production
and distribution, which measures the human reality in dollars and cents. Both social
thinkers, Scheler and Mannheim, understood the relativism promoted by positivistic social science as a method that detached observers from their moral responses, prevented them from reacting hu-
manly to the topic under study, and en-
couraged a passive stand toward history.
Relativism, in the eyes of Scheler and
Mannheim, was a dangerous human attitude that would eventually turn into skepticism and its product, social apathy. They
held that skepticism was easily available
in a successful class that had lost the sense
of its own destiny and relativized its own
values with a shrug of the shoulders.

There is another form of relativism
against which Scheler and Mannheim had

to wrestle. It came from an intellectual tradition which had influenced Scheler and with which Mannheim largely identified himself, although in a qualified way, an intellectual tradition partly derived from German idealism and partly from German historiography, which is called *Historismus* in German and which is almost inevitably but misleadingly translated into English as "historicism."[12] "Historism" just does not sound well in English. This German historicism recognized the historical character of human life: society is what it is because of its history and the human mind is what it is because of its history. Each society, each culture, is in some way an historically produced totality, and the social scientist must try to understand the lives of the people in it in concepts generated by their own self-understanding and interpret the details of this society, or this culture, in terms of its totality. Social scientists must take heed lest they introduce their own socially and/or culturally defined ideas and categories in their study of the social world distinct from their own.

Scientists must even abstract from their own views of right and wrong, good and evil. Historicists readily admit that within each totality people develop criteria to distinguish truth from falsehood and good from evil: to these criteria the social scientists must pay attention. But these criteria depend on their social foundation; they are not and cannot be universal.

The historicist approach manifests humility. The social scientist respects the other culture, refuses to impose her own categories, and seeks to understand what norms of truth and action are operative in it. And in this historicism differs considerably from positivism. But in the long run, because it recognizes a plurality of truths, historicism leads to relativism. This is what happened to Wilhelm Dilthey toward the end of his life. The cultural visions possible in human history may be few in number; still, it is impossible to choose among them by any rational criterion. And since no transhistorical norm can be found relating the various cultures to one another, historicists easily turn to a voluntarist under-

standing of truth and values. A triumphant
culture makes its truth superior; by assert-
ing itself in history in political terms, it
gives its values universal meaning. While
all cultures are admirable human creations
and as such deserve equal respect, German
historicists have been willing to recognize
special moments in history when a particular society is called to assume a leading
role, exercise a special task in humanity,
and assign its norms and values a special
predominance. Even respectable German
thinkers at the turn of the century thought
that the German nation, with its German
culture, its science and its historical understanding of the human reality, was called
upon to exercise special leadership in the
world and extend its political power. The
nation at this special hour, summoned by
the circumstances, is not bound by ordinary morality proper to a previous stage of
history. Its political and spiritual self-
affirmation creates, as it were, its own
superior morality. Scheler and Mannheim
opposed the relativism proper to historicism because they feared that it might

undermine common human norms elaborated over the centuries and legitimate a voluntarist, power-political morality.

In this lecture, I want to deal with Mannheim's effort to overcome historicist relativism by means of the sociology of knowledge. Mannheim, as we shall see, places himself in line with historicism and, following Troeltsch, wants to transcend history by history.[13] Scheler followed a different tack altogether. Scheler tried to affirm at one and the same time the historically generated nature of socio-cultural unities and hence also the historically generated nature of the human mind, and—beyond these historical determinations and undergirding them—the existence of absolute values. Scheler tried to combine radical sociology of knowledge which refuses to understand ideas and ideals without taking into consideration their social location and radical Platonism which affirmed the existence of absolute norms beyond history, including the supreme norm, the holy, the living God. Scheler's brilliant writings dazzle the reader: he is a radical on both sides of the spectrum. The question that has not been answered satisfactorily is whether the two poles of his thought really hold together. The ruling metaphor which Scheler uses in his writings on the relative and absolute nature of truth is the mountain range which appears different from different locations in the plain but which remains identical with itself, despite its different profiles. For Scheler the sociology of knowledge was an attempt to reconcile the different socially determined perspectives, dependent on ethnic heritage, cultural tradition and social location, in a single trans-historical truth, a process which pushed him through various intermediary stages to theology, to the affirmation of a divine Logos operating within the creation of diverse cultures and styles of thought. It was his great metaphysical confidence, grounded in deep, though ever-restless religious conviction, that made Scheler defend the view that despite the historicity of the human mind, there is a wisdom that transcends the social dependency of truth and attains to trans-historical values.

The weakness and, I think, the inconsistency of Max Scheler's position lies in his presupposition of the radical separation of the knowing subject and the known object, prior to the act of knowledge. The observer and the mountain range are separate entities brought together in the act of seeing. Yet this antecedent separation between subject and object does not render an adequate account of what we have called the historicity of the mind. According to historicism and the sociology of knowledge, a human mind is not a given, a universally identical thinking organism, which faces the world of things and human beings: the human mind, rather, is constituted by an historical process, its modes of thought defined by particular cultural identifications. In many, if not most, cases, the objects which this human mind encounters and seeks to know have, prior to the act of knowledge, been part of the mind's own history and affected its very constitution. In some sense, therefore, the object known pre-exists in the knowing

subject. The antecedent radical separation
of object and subject is an illusion.

If we consider that the object of the
social sciences is also historically constituted, we must say that in many, if not
most, cases the subject and the object have
been produced by the same historical
process. The mind has become what it is
by encountering the social reality it now
seeks to study in detail, while this social
reality has been constituted by a process
which has been affected by the observer
and his world. The white social scientist
studying the behaviour of black people is
a useful example: the mind of the observer
has been shaped by a history in which the
black people had a role, and in turn the
behaviour of black people has a history
which is strongly affected by the white
man's world. To suppose a radical antecedent separation of subject and object
would lead to gravely biased results. What
the researcher has to clarify for himself in
setting up his research project is the antecedent historical interrelationship. It is
true, of course, that if a researcher moves

to a foreign culture which never acted upon, and was never affected by, his own cultural world, then there is a considerable antecedent separation of subject and object. But the researcher can make meaningful observations and reach some understanding only after he has lived in the new culture for a while, after the observer and the observed have interacted and affected one another, after they have shared some common experiences. It is again the common history that provides the entry into the knowledge of the distant culture.

Max Scheler forgets, we repeat, that observer and the mountain range, i.e., the section of history observed, are produced by the same historical process. Hence, in some sense, the object is in the subject; and since even the object has come to be the way it is through a process affected by the subject and the subject's people, class or group, it is equally correct to say that the subject exists in the object. (The mountain range analogy does not even apply to man's perception of the divine. For the mystery of God is never simply a reality

facing man as supreme value but is also
and especially the presupposition and
foundation of human being, human knowing and human loving.) It is impossible,
therefore, to follow Scheler's reconciliation
of relativity and transcendence.

Karl Mannheim enjoyed no such metaphysical confidence. What he wanted to
do, therefore, was to struggle against posi-
tivist and historicist relativism by remaining faithful to the basic insights of the
sociology of knowledge. How is it possible
to transcend history and reach truth that
is universally valid? To facilitate his sociological reflections, Mannheim distinguished between *relativism* and *relationism*.[14] Relativism is the approach that recognizes that all knowledge is socially dependent, bound to the location of the
thinker, and reasons from this to the inevitable relativity of all human truth. Relationism, on the other hand, is the approach that also acknowledges the social
dependency of knowledge but refuses to
use this principle reductively as an argument for the relativity of all truth. What

exactly does Mannheim's relationism stand for? Many social philosophers have suggested that Mannheim's distinction is meaningless: they have argued that he does not provide an adequate account of how to transcend historically dependent knowledge and that his account of relationism does not really make it distinct from relativism. This is the question I wish to pursue in this lecture. I shall follow Mannheim in his reflections, but basing myself on hints and remarks made in passing, I wish to move a little beyond him and indicate how it is possible, in line with the sociology of knowledge, to transcend the social dependency of truth.

Mannheim begins his clarification of relationism by examining the nature of truth, especially truth in the human sciences (*Geisteswissenschaft*). If $2+2=4$ is accepted as the model of truth, then it is inevitable that the social dependency of truth leads to relativism and the rejection of transhistorical truth. Then the existence of many truths means that they are all equally questionable. The $2+2=4$ model of truth may apply to the natural sciences; at least it appears to many scientists that it does, and if they are correct, then science may indeed reach truths of universal validity. But when it comes to the human sciences the sociology of knowledge demands the application of a more dynamic understanding of truth. Why? Because if it is correct that the knowledge of the human reality is socially dependent, then the scholar recognizes that his position, however carefully researched, documented, tested and accepted by his peers, is only one perspective, determined by his and his colleagues' social location, and hence is in need of complementation by other perspectives available from other social locations. Truth stands in need of complementation, correction and expansion. Truth, dynamically understood, retains an openness to other socially defined viewpoints. Mannheim calls this "openness to totality."[15]

This sociology of knowledge approach in no way weakens the scientific, logical rigour of research and reflection; it does not dispense scholars from the effort to free themselves from biases due to their class and culture; it does not reduce the effort of scholars to arrive at "objective" results where "objective" means that the results stand up under the criticism of the scholarly community. Still, if concepts and ideas are dependent on the social location of the thinker, then this so-called "objectivity" is only partial, is from one perspective alone, and must remain open to being complemented, modified and expanded by many other perspectives. Thus white social thinkers studying the social reality of America will welcome the contribution of black researchers, knowing that without some correction and complementation their own work will remain too one-sided. Thus male researchers will remain open to the scholarly work done by women researchers. Thus American historians will remain open to the Canadian perspective. And the thinkers identified with the Western historical tradition will recognize the partial nature of their insights and remain open to the perspectives of other cultures.

(Allow me to mention in passing that from the viewpoint of the sociology of knowledge the practice in the Catholic Church that the moral norms for sexual behaviour are formulated for people in all parts of the world by a group of males dedicated to sexual continence is somewhat ludicrous and based on an inadequate concept of truth.)

The dynamic understanding of truth, which we shall explore in greater detail below, is for Mannheim a logical implication of the sociology of knowledge and its first principle, the social dependency of truth. He formulates the following equations:

social dependency of truth + static view of truth = relativism

social dependency of truth + dynamic view of truth = relationism

These equations affirm that if one accepts the dynamic view of truth, implicit in the sociology of knowledge, then the social dependency of truth does not lead to relativism.

The openness of truth to totality has no

limits. Social thinkers will want to be open to the insights of the past, they will want to listen to the research and ideas produced today in social locations culturally or politically other than their own, and they will want to remain open to future developments. The dynamic notion of truth, then, implies that truth in its final and universal sense can only be affirmed at the end of history, only when all the perspectives have come in. We recognize that we may be overlooking significant elements of human existence at this time: only the experience of cultures yet to come or the self-expression of groups until now condemned to silence may uncover them for us. The women's movement of our day is a good example of the emergence of a new perspective, catching social scientists, philosophers and theologians by surprise, which demands a radical re-thinking of values, institutions and ideas that were previously regarded as soundly based in the order of the universe. The sociology of knowledge summons forth an expectant, open-ended view of truth.

Mannheim makes a few very important remarks which suggest a hidden connection between this "openness to totality" and political orientation. The perspective under which we examine the object of research depends on the social location of the scholar, but within this location he can adopt various stances. For Mannheim it is quite clear that these stances are related to the scholar's personal social vision and political commitment. The manner in which we perceive ourselves in our own historical situation and visualize society as it ought to be affects the manner in which we perceive the object of our research. Mannheim follows here a basic principle of historiography: history must always be rewritten. Why? Because when people move to a new historical context, they are confronted by new problems, they formulate their hopes in new ways; they reread the past from a new perspective, discover aspects of the past they had previously overlooked, and learn to see in their history a movement that helps them, in the new situation, to meet the challenges of life. Associated with every truth perspective is a socio-political stance which is either due to the scholar's unconscious identification with the cultural outlook of her class or a consciously chosen attitude. We shall examine this action-oriented aspect of truth further on. What is important for us at this point is that implicit in the dynamic concept of truth, or the openness of truth to totality, is what Mannheim calls "a political élan,"[16] a political aspiration toward a social order in which the complementation, modification and expansion of perspectival truth is possible.

Mannheim only makes a few hints in regard to this political élan. In our own day, Jürgen Habermas has clarified these hints.[17] The discovery of truth in its totality must take place in a dialogue in which the various sections of humanity—cultures, classes and races—listen to and learn from one another, and such a dialogue demands the equality of partners. True dialogue takes place only among equals. There is no dialogue across the boundary between masters and servants, for the master will

listen only as long as his power remains
intact and the servant will limit his communication to utterances for which he cannot be punished. In fact, to recommend
dialogue in a situation of inequality of
power is a deceptive ideology of the powerful, who wish to persuade the powerless
that harmony and mutual understanding
are possible in society without any change
in the status quo of power. The openness
of truth to totality, then, implies a political
élan that fosters significant social change
in the distribution of power and the aboli-
tion of the master/servant relationships in
the human family: a commitment to emancipation.

This result is startling. But what does
political élan have to do with truth? In
the view of Mannheim, all knowledge is
carried by an intentionality. He derived
this position from two sources, phenomen-
ology and the Marxist philosophy of history. We seek knowledge in order to
achieve something; we affirm ourselves in
knowledge; by knowing we deal with the
world, we solve our problems, we wrestle

against our enemies. Looked upon from this wider perspective, knowledge is part of world building and hence, like action, an element in man's creation of man.

But before we explore the action-oriented character of knowledge any further we must ask what intentionality was operative in the creation of the sociology of knowledge. What socio-political aim made Scheler, and more particularly Mannheim, reach out for a position that accepted the pluriformity of truth and yet repudiated cognitive and ethical relativism? We have already made a few remarks on this topic. Here I wish to mention an intentionality intrinsic to the exercise of sociology.

If modes of thought and their truth are relative and cannot transcend the culture in which they are produced, how can the social sciences lay claim to universal validity? If there were complete relativism of ideas, university departments of sociology and anthropology would have to close their doors. Why do scholars have the confidence to cross the ocean and study a dis-

tant culture with methods proper to their
own? Why do students of history believe
that they can do critical research on the
past and gain some understanding of what
took place then? The human sciences pre-
suppose that there is a common ground
between different cultures and different
ages, which makes communication and
understanding possible. There is something common in all human collectivities,
whatever their concrete circumstances,
which seems to transcend their historical
situation. Some philosophers invoke here
a common "human nature": they hold that
this is the foundation for the universality
of the human sciences. But from the perspective of the sociology of knowledge, it
is impossible to speak of a common "human
nature" since human mind and human nature are historically constituted; if there
is a common ground between people
everywhere which enables social scientists
to regard their methods as having universal validity, then this common ground is
produced by the historical process itself.

It is not difficult to spell out what these

specifically human common experiences
are. The biological basis of human life
and man's slow acquisition of consciousness account for the common human experiences of entering life as a helpless in-
fant, being dependent on parents and
parent figures, and then by a turbulent
process, becoming relatively independent
of them, a drama which has been studied
by Sigmund Freud and his followers.
While the family structure may differ
greatly from culture to culture, the passage
from infancy to independence has common elements which constitute a bridge
between peoples everywhere. This universal drama, summed up by Herbert
Marcuse under the name of "basic repres-
sion" (to distinguish it from surplus re-
pression imposed by society) constitutes a
common source of memories, dreams and
symbols that lay the foundation for communication between cultures. That is why
we love one another's poetry. Yet there
are other common bonds. Again, thanks
to man's biological base, people produce
tools for the procuring of food and shelter

and institutions for dealing with their collective needs, and while these may differ greatly from one culture to another, they have a certain similarity, serving needs based on the same biology, and hence constitute a common ground upon which conversation is possible. There is no need to postulate a common "human nature" to found the universal conversation between peoples.

This common ground, we note, is continually extended by ongoing conversation and cooperation. A scholar studying a distant culture will hesitate to apply the categories derived from her own cultural experience to understand the social action of people remote from her own history. But since there is enough common ground to start with, researchers and members of the remote culture are able to have some exchange, share certain experiences, establish some sort of communication, until eventually, once the common ground has been extended, the scholar may be able to interpret the cultural life and political organizations of these people in terms of their own collective self-understanding.

We have here one limit of relativism. The basic needs of human life constitute a set of common values operative in all cultures, however different their concrete forms: it is better to eat than to be hungry, it is better to be comfortable than to be wet and cold, it is better to be with friends than to be isolated, it is better to be loved than to be rejected, etc. Yet these common experiences do not constitute "human nature": human nature remains unfinished.

Sociology in its exercise cannot refrain from value judgments. In fact, Scheler and Mannheim vehemently opposed the idea of a value-free social science. They regarded value-neutral social science as an illusion: the claim to objectivity merely disguises the scholar's identification with the dominant culture and his research will accordingly tend to protect and legitimate the dominant culture. But where do we turn to values that transcend the social order and have universal validity? Scheler, as I mentioned above, went the way of metaphysics. Mannheim wanted to avoid this. He confronted the dilemma of the social scientists who on the one hand want to understand social action from within, from the viewpoint of the actors' self-understanding, but who on the other hand desire to gain a normative understanding of it.

For many social scientists this is not a dilemma. Many are quite content to produce studies of social action, however destructive in terms of the function it plays in creating a stable society. To give an instance, we can find studies of the witch hunts of the 17th century that understand this gruesome social phenomenon in terms of its contribution to greater stability by settling the anxiety of the population and strengthening the necessary consensus. Radicals cannot do this. Radicals must judge evil and oppressive behaviour. Radicals are convinced that there are norms and values transcending their own social background, which allow them to perceive other societies in terms of the conflict between good and evil. This is true of religious radicals. The prophets of

Israel and Jesus Christ announced norms of justice applicable to all nations. But this is equally true of secular radicals. Karl Marx believed that his analysis of class oppression was in some sense applicable to all societies: his message of overcoming human self-alienation had something to say wherever people live. And this was true of Freud as well. He also held, possibly quite falsely, that his analysis of the infancy drama, the oedipal complex, accounted not only for the pathology of western culture but could also be applied in the diagnosis and healing of people from other cultures. Radicals are convinced that evil and suffering have marked the whole of human life, and they yearn for the remedy: they hold that their analysis of evil, their plan for overcoming it, their message to the people—have universal significance. Radicals are convinced that there is a difference between right and wrong, and that the violation of this distinction makes the world a place of misery. In this sense, then, Mannheim was a radical.

We noted that Mannheim shied away
from regarding "human nature" as a universal norm. While he recognized certain
common human features and even values—
we mentioned this above—he refused to
speak of human nature as if it had been
fully constituted. Mannheim accepted the
Marxian critique that "human nature" is
the self-understanding of the dominant
class. The successful class in the successful culture regards itself as the measure
of the human reality and invests its own
self-understanding with normative power.
Hence the definitions of human nature
cannot be trusted. Human nature still has
to be produced through the historical
process, based on participation, on equal
footing, of all sections of humanity.

In this connection it is interesting to
note the recent change in the definition of
human nature in the Catholic tradition. At
one time Catholic teachers, endorsed by
the official church, taught that the subordination of women to the male members
of the species belonged to the order of the
universe. Women were by nature men's

associates and helpers. The regular exercise of leadership in the community would be unnatural for women. While supernaturally, in view of Christ's redemption, men and women were equals, they were unequal by nature and hence even in the church, the supernatural society, women were unable to exercise positions of leadership and be bearers of sacramental power. In a recent church document, we find a modified definition of human nature.[18] We are told that human nature does not define the subordination of women to the male members of the species and hence women are by no means barred from exercising leadership positions in society. This new view is obviously related to the actual social change that has taken place in Western society: it dawned upon theologians only after women have become conscious of their inferior position, organized a movement to change the structure of society, and achieved considerable success. What is very curious, and interesting from the viewpoint of the sociology of knowledge, is that while the recent church docu-

ment, in contrast with previous teaching,
affirms the equality of men and women in
the order of nature, it now places the ob-
stacle for the ordination of women in the
order of the supernatural and claims what
the Catholic tradition has never done, that
the priest must be created in the image of
Jesus' maleness.

For Karl Mannheim, human nature re-
mained as yet incomplete. The unity of the
human race was not a given, except in certain common conditions, enough as a start-
ing point for communication and cooperation. Until now the human race is still
seriously torn by an unequal distribution
of power and the wounds that oppression
inflicts on the servants as well as the
masters. It is the destiny of men and
women to struggle for the creation of a
single human family, and by doing so produce the conditions for the defining of a
common human nature.

Where does the social passion of radical
thinkers, such as Mannheim, come from?
Is it simply due to the experience of belonging to a disadvantaged group? Mann-

heim, like Marx, came from a Jewish background: he knew what marginalization
meant. Yet this experience alone cannot
account for the radicalism of which I
speak. It seems to me that experiences of
oppression give rise to a radical, universal-
ist commitment only if they become the
key for the understanding of the struggle
in the entire world. Oppression can produce anger, revolt or revenge—or passivity
and compliance. But in order to experience
oppression as a source of radicalism, in the
sense in which I use the term, one's personal experience must become the symbol
of a wider interpretation of human life.
The concrete struggle for freedom here
reveals—and I use the word "reveal" ad-
visedly—the meaning of the entire history.
Christians can become radicals by identi-
fying with the marginalized Jesus. Mannheim was a secular man who had left religion behind. Yet the theologian finds it
difficult to account for a radical passion
such as his, against the flow of his own
elitist culture, without relating it to the
divine call operative in history in a hidden

way.

This discussion has clarified the intentionality behind the sociology of knowledge. I mentioned earlier that Mannheim regarded all knowledge as carried by an intentionality: knowledge had a purpose, knowledge was part of world building. For Scheler it was only science, natural science and social science to the extent that it was assimilated to the scientific method, that were carried forward by a world building intention: according to Scheler, as mentioned earlier, science and technology were bent on domination, an intentionality dangerous to human beings in the long run. Metaphysics and religion were not intent on world building: here people were in touch with truth and the sacred beyond the requirements of their earthly situation. With greater consistency Mannheim followed the Marxian view that people create the tools for producing food, shelter and the satisfaction of material needs, and by doing so constitute their own consciousness. The mental and symbolic world of consciousness is not a simple reflection of the material base, as vulgar Marxism[19] suggests, but it is a reflection in which there is room for the independent creativity of persons. Social determination, as we saw many times before, is not defined against personal freedom. Still, the production of ideas and of the whole of culture is part of the world building process, and from this point of view is not that different from action. Thought is grounded in action, proceeds from a consciousness dependent on the social location of the thinker, tries to deal with the problems posed to the group (and sometimes to thinkers individually), thus steering them to a certain way of perceiving the social reality and acting in it. Thought, whether scientific, metaphysical or religious, is grounded in action and in turn leads to action, and no adequate understanding of an idea is possible, unless these two aspects, the "whence" and the "whither" of thought, are taken seriously. When we dealt above with the situatedness of knowledge we only looked at the first aspect; now we expand our consideration and include in the historicity of ideas also their concrete effect on the building of the world. Knowledge has a value-orientation. It is impossible to call an idea true in the dynamic sense of the word unless one is ready to co-affirm the world which it creates. We cannot know the truth unless we are oriented toward a human, non-devouring society.

But what precisely is the kind of world we are called upon to build? Is there some way of specifying a common goal for all human societies? This is precisely the difficulty. For if all ideas and values are founded upon particular historical experience, how then can we find a universal norm? How can we transcend history from within history? We have already seen that Mannheim argued that the openness of truth to totality implied a political élan toward the emancipation of the human race. What this means in concrete situations is, of course, still unsolved. Unless we are able to indicate procedures for transcending culture-bound and class-bound ideals, we have not solved the problem.

We note in passing that Mannheim's idea of "dynamic truth" renders an account of the relationship between theory and practice that differs considerably from that of classical philosophy. The relation of truth to action is intrinsic to thought itself. The perspective in which observers look upon the social reality under study is determined by their social location as well as by their political élan. Their commitment to what society ought to be influences their definition of the question to be studied, determines their selection of data, shapes the sensitivity with which they read the data, and influences their choice of conceptual tools employed in the process of understanding. Truth is not discovered by thinkers on neutral ground, and then applied to a particular situation. Truth is available as we perceive the world through an emancipatory commitment, and then its application is the proper prolongation of the thought.

Social science must be "objective" in the sense that scholars seek detachment from bias and prejudice due to cultural back-

ground, present their findings with the
evidence and the reasoning that support
them, and submit them to be tested by
their colleagues and eventually by the
whole community of scholars. However,
social sciences are not detached, not
value-free, which means that scholars must
clarify for themselves what their socio-
political ideals are and, if need be, to ad-
just them so that their perspective is truly
open to universality and the emancipation
implicit in it. This defines a new objectivity for the social sciences.

We now come to the important question: how are we able to transcend the
social dependency of truth and move
toward more universal ideas and values?
Mannheim is able to deal with this question because for him the quest for knowledge is a collective undertaking before it
is private research. Mannheim recognizes,
following the sociology of Max Weber,
that in every society there are dominant
classes and authoritative institutions, up-
held by a culture produced by them, —and
there are lower and marginal strata. Every

society is stratified. From the lower strata the society presents an image that is quite different from its self-understanding produced and communicated by the dominant culture. From the lower strata become visible the weaknesses, injustices and contradictions that remain hidden from those identified with the dominant structures. The modes of thought accepted by a culture and the social virtues recommended by it have an ugly underside that is discoverable by the inferiorised groups. People of the lower strata express their protest against the world that oppresses them in religious or secular symbols of various kinds, and when they gain access to learning they are able to develop modes of thought and advocate values that transcend the dominant culture. Culturally transcendent perceptions usually emerge in marginal movements, like the movement started by Jesus of Nazareth, that are repudiated by the defenders of the dominant structures and survive only by remaining partially underground. Transcendence does not emerge in the offices of tenured professors nor does it arise in chancery offices. Transcendence has always demanded a price, like the pearl of great value.

To spark these countervailing movements in society popular leaders are required, men Max Weber called "charismatic," who are able to put into words the frustrations which people suffer and provide a new imagination, which Mannheim calls "utopian," of how society ought to be. The transcedence of the present order takes place first of all in the utopian imagination of gifted people and the countervailing movements sparked by them. Mannheim believed—and he was criticized by many radical social thinkers for this— that utopias (like ideologies) present a distorted perception of the social reality. Utopias are in need of correction; they too must be "open to totality"; they too stand in need of complementation, correction and expansion. Still, without a utopia operative at some level of the social order, society remains fixed, unchanging, linked to the ideas, values and institutions proper to the dominant structures. Without utopias there is no transcendence.[20]

This topic demands a careful analysis. In an important chapter of his *Ideology and Utopia* Mannheim examines the important utopias that have emerged in European history, some of which have been crushed while others, especially the liberal utopia of the bourgeoisie struggling against aristocracy, have been enormously successful and have become the dominant ideology of the Western nations. What utopias are operative in the present age? Mannheim does not reveal his mind completely here. He repudiates the form of Marxism he encountered in the nineteen-twenties. He rejects the religious utopias that still move many people. But since he advocates a concept of truth that remains open to totality and envisages a society in which all sectors are in ongoing conversation, his utopia seems to be emancipation of the human race.

Mannheim makes a point that is important for theology: he shows that the transcendence of ideas bound to culture and class does not become available simply with a reference to an absolute, even if this be God. In some situations, a reference to the divinity may in fact protect the ideas and values of the dominant class and tie people more deeply into the categories of a once powerful group that is now threatened to lose its hegemony.[21]

The first move, then, in overcoming the social dependency of knowledge is to listen to the oppressed. In the voice of the dominated strata of society a truth perspective emerges that is inaccessible to the dominant culture. For Mannheim, this listening remains a critical intellectual process. By an identification with the lower stratum, a perspective becomes available to scholars which remains otherwise hidden and which complements, corrects and expands the dominant wisdom of society. The effect of the women's movement on the theological understanding of human nature is a good example: male thinkers were unable to perceive the one-sidedness of their own perception until they permitted themselves to be affected by the voice of women or, in other cases, until they lived in social conditions which were in fact defined in terms of greater equality between the sexes. Some persons are so strongly identified with the dominant structure, either by their position of power, the conditions of employment, or some other interests, that they are incapable of listening to the voice of the subjugated. They remain enclosed in the inherited ideas and values. They cannot affirm the openness of truth to totality. But there are other persons in society who can free themselves from the dominant ideology, either because they themselves belong to a subjugated group or because they are members of a social network that is largely independent of the dominant structure and hence are able, if they so choose, to identify with the perspective of the oppressed. Through these persons, usually a minority, society remains open to transcendence.

At one time Mannheim thought that for historical reasons the German intellectuals constituted a free-floating network, free to

identify themselves with the various sections of society, including the most exploited, and were for this reason the ideal
mediators in society between the aspira-
tions of the various groups.[22] Some sociologists have given this view great promi-
nence, have presented it as an essential
part of his sociology of knowledge, and
then have rejected it as blindly optimistic.
In fact Mannheim does not attach much
importance to his remarks on intellectuals
in *Ideology and Utopia*. What is true is that
people employed as teachers, professors,
social workers and so forth, who make a
living in relative distance from the com-
petitive economic world, often have an
ideal of cooperation and dedication, one
they encounter in their profession, from
which they criticize the dominant economic system and derive great sympathy
for the radical critique of society offered
by oppressed minorities. These teachers,
professors and social workers may be a
minority in their profession, but when we
study the countervailing movements bent
on creating a more just society we find

this minority has often played a significant part. What counts for us at this point is that it is possible for persons in society, even when surrounded by privilege, to open themselves to the perspective of the oppressed and overcome the cognitive limitations of their own social connection.

The major churches have on the whole been identified with the dominant classes in society.[23] Still, there have always emerged persons in the church with a fairly loose relationship to the ecclesiastical apparatus who were able to listen to the voice of the humiliated and marginalized Jesus, to his persecution, capital punishment and resurrection, and thus acquire a perspective on reality that made it possible for them to overcome the concepts and ideals proper to their religious and secular culture. According to the Mannheimian principles, the cross provides a perspective of transcendence. The Christian message has again and again enabled believers to identify with "the poor," listen to their voice, and detect in their experience a truth hidden from the dominant culture and the ruling élite.

These Christians, I wish to add, will want to speak of God in a politically responsible manner. They realize that a divinity conceived as lord who produced and now protects the existing social order with its injustice, is not transcendent at all, however high one may make the metaphysical claims. Divinity is transcendent when it actually judges the existing order, condemns the injustices of the social system, and empowers those unjustly treated to struggle for the remaking of society according to greater justice. According to the sociology of knowledge, a doctrine of God is an ideological defense of the *status quo* and bespeaks no transcendence whatever, unless it is open to totality and based on a commitment to universal liberation. Emancipation, we noted, was only a utopian vision for Mannheim, thanks to which mankind moved toward greater humanization. For Christians, emancipation is linked to the divine promises. The redemption at work in creation, revealed in Jesus Christ, and oriented by the Spirit to its fullness, delivers people from all the enemies of human life, including the conditions of oppression.[24]

We now come to the second move in the overcoming of the social dependency of knowledge, which is dialogue. The openness of truth to totality demands an ongoing conversation with people who see the world from a different location. If their historical place is one of oppression, then it is necessary to listen to them—we have covered this in the previous section—but if their place in history is at a level relatively equal with ourselves, then we must engage in dialogue. Partners in dialogue may belong to a past age, or to a parallel culture, or to groups within our own society. Mannheim never uses the word "dialogue," but he renders a very precise account of it. In fact, he proposes the sociology of knowledge as a methodology for dialogue.[25] When we listen to the public position of others, what counts is not only to understand what they say; it is equally necessary to relate their position to its social foundation and thus discover what their core concern is. We have to listen not only to what others say but also to what they mean—and this latter may differ considerably from the former. The core concern in many instances may be more limited, more circumscribed, than the public affirmation in which it is expressed. While our own position may be clearly at odds with the public affirmation of the others, it may be closer to their core concern. In fact, if we use a sociology of knowledge approach to discover what core concern, what intentionality, stands behind our own position, we might be able to produce a new formulation of our conviction, one that takes care of our own core concern and is closer to the core concern of the others. The clarification of the intentionality of ideas brings the two parties closer together and opens both of them to transcendence. Without reprehensible compromise the consensus has been widened: truth becomes more universal.

Mannheim believed that the modern world had created the social conditions

that made dialogue possible—and in fact
necessary. Because of social upheaval and
growing industrialization, Germany following World War I was deeply divided
among different groups that held seem-
ingly irreconcilable world views and yet
were obliged to produce a consensus that
made social life possible. Germany was
here the symbol of the modern world.
Social upheaval, industrialization and the
shrinking of the globe bring together different cultures and diverse societies so that
dialogue becomes possible and in fact necessary. Since all peoples will have to build
a common home on this small globe, it is
imperative that they engage in dialogue
and arrive at a common wisdom. Dialogue
enables social thinkers to transcend the
social dependency of knowledge and without infidelity to the core concerns of their
own culture move toward a new, more universal position. The cooperation and conversation between peoples must eventually
constitute the process whereby humanity
will become truly one. It is clearly impossible to bridge the differences between

cultures and groups by an effort of the mind: the bridging of the difference must take place first of all in common action, in constituting a common history, and—parallel with this—in dialogue reaching out for wider consensus. As we mentioned several times, we must construct the unity of the human family before we will be able to formulate truth and values in a manner that is truly universal.

As listening to the oppressed demands commitment to their liberation, so dialogue demands commitment to solidarity. We recognize ourselves as citizens of the same globe, although members of distinct communities; we are interdependent on one another; we are together responsible for our common future; we are bound to build a common humanity. We note that the first and the second move in overcoming the dependency of knowledge are interrelated, for we must construct a common humanity out of peoples, many of whom have been oppressed. Commitment to emancipation is joined to the commitment to solidarity. From this political élan we are able to cross boundaries, reach out to others, build a common world, and in this way transcend the social dependency of truth.

Where do we ground the reliability of human knowledge? Where do we find the measure that protects us from relativism and enables knowledge to be shared by all? What is the test of truth? For the classical realist philosophers, the measure of truth was the objective world. The reality confronting the mind, understood as self-identical, assured the existence of a common truth. Truth in this context meant the conformity of the mind to the object. In Kantian and neo-Kantian philosophy the stability of truth is situated in the subject. Since the human mind has an identical structure everywhere, it founds the universality of scientific knowledge. The test for truth is the fidelity to the working of the mind. Truth in this context refers to the authenticity of the subject seeking knowledge. Mannheim rejected both measures of universal truth, for both the object and the subject were historically consti-

tuted and hence could not be the stable
foundation for the universality of truth.
He proposed that the measure of truth is
derived neither from the object nor the
subject but from the world which the inter-
action of object and subject create. Knowledge, as we saw above, is action-oriented;
it is part of the world building process. The
test of truth is the world it creates. Knowledge is true (in the dynamic sense defined by Mannheim) when it moves history closer to emancipation and solidarity.

Before concluding this lecture, I wish
to make a few remarks on Christian theology. Mannheim did not believe in God;
he entertained a wholly secular perspective, and hence there is a radical difference between his sociology of knowledge
approach and the Christian theological
perspective. At the same time Mannheim
realized that implicit in his theory were
metaphysical assumptions, but he pre-
ferred not to deal with them.[26] Presup-

posed in his analysis of the historical process seems to be a trust in a certain dynamic rationality operative in human beings which carries them forward and makes possible the striving for emancipation and solidarity. Mannheim did not claim to know whether the human race would actually move in this direction, but he recognized in the human world the preconditions that made such a development possible. And since he himself dedicated his life to this, he was carried by some hope that the common striving was not based on an empty dream.

Christians believe in divine revelation, and hence they are able to render an account of the hope that is within them. What is of interest to us here is that there is a growing trend in Catholic theology that understands God as the transcendent mystery, present to the world as ground, orientation and horizon, which has revealed itself in Israel and in Jesus Christ as the redemption of the human race. In Jesus, God's hidden presence has been made known. God is the mystery that sum-

mons people to recognize the personal and
social sins that destroy their lives, shakes
them free from the inherited categories
and institutions, empowers them to stand
together and remake the world in accord-
ance with greater justice. God liberates
men and women from the destructive past
to enter a more reconciled and truly human future. God is the forward movement
in history. God is operative among people
as they overcome the blindness of their
culture, long for a more humane world,
engage in action to reconstruct their society, and transcend their personal and
collective egoism. God's self-communica-
tion takes place at the heart of the historical process. Modern theology tries to find
non-dualistic language for speaking of
God's relationship to the world. God's in-
finity is not over and above the finite; the
infinite is in and through the finite as its
unfolding forward movement. God's transcendence is not, as it were, at right angles
to the flow of history; divine transcendence
is rather situated at the heart of creation,
making people capable of transcending the

limited and sinful conditions of their personal and collective lives. Theologians who follow this new approach will have some sympathy for Mannheim's sociological theory.

In this contemporary theological perspective, divine revelation in Jesus Christ is not new truth uttered into the world from a superior realm: divine revelation rather makes known to people the hidden redemptive presence of God in their lives. Faith in God's Word initiates believers into a new consciousness; they perceive the world in a new way, become capable of transcending its categories, orient themselves toward a new solidarity, and begin to act out of a new vision. The Christian message offers salvation. Truth redeems. "The truth shall make you free." We have here a notion of truth that is action-oriented and dynamic. To understand the meaning and power of Christian teaching we must relate it to the concrete historical situation in which it was uttered and then ask what consciousness it created and what action it evoked. If truth is redemp-

tive, then the test of Christian truth is not
the conformity to an unchanging conceptual norm, but the freeing, redeeming,
transforming action that flows from it. The
test of truth is the new life.

These are a few theological hints that
would demand careful systematic attention. The theological approach described
above creates a perspective in which
Mannheim's sociology of knowledge could
be usefully applied. It may be possible to
render an account of the pluralism within
the Christian tradition. For in each people,
in each historical age, in each new situation in which sin and evil acquire new
proportions, it is necessary to proclaim the
identical Gospel in different ways. The
ancient Christian creeds must be made to
say different things in different situations
so that they promote the identical orientation toward universal redemption in these
diverse environments. Universal redemption includes emancipation and solidarity.
There is no reason, then, why theologians,
while remaining faithful to God's revelation in Jesus Christ, could not use Mann-

heim's sociology of knowledge to render
a theological account of the church's
changing teaching, giving witness to a
single, self-identical Gospel.

1. Vatican Council II, *Gaudium et spes* 44.

2. Emil Fackenheim, *Metaphysics and Historicity* (The Aquinas Lectures; Milwaukee: Marquette U. Press, 1961.)

3. Karl Mannheim, *Ideology and Utopia* (Harvest Books: New York: Harcourt, Brace & World, n.d.). This work, first published in German in 1929, was translated into English by L. Wirth and E. Shils and published in the United States in 1936. Subsequent references are to the Harvest Books edition.

4. Karl Marx, *Selected Writings* (ed. T. B. Bottomore; New York: McGraw-Hill, 1964) p. 75.

5. Cf. G. Radnitzky, *Continental Schools of Metascience* (Göteborg: Akademiförlaget, 1968) pp. 26-30.

6. Mannheim, *Ideology and Utopia,* pp. 5-12.

7. Max Scheler, "Probleme einer Soziologie des Wissens," *Die Wissenschaftsformen und die Gesellschaft* (Bern: Francke Verlag, 1960) pp. 135-57.

8. Ibid., p. 29. Cf. also his "Moralia," *Schriften zur Soziologie und Weltanschauungslehre* (Bern: Francke Verlag, 1963) pp. 27-35.

9. Karl Mannheim, "On the Interpretation of 'Weltanschauung,'" *Essays on the Sociology of Knowledge* (London: Routledge & Kegan Paul, 1952) pp. 43-63.

10. Pierre Thibault, *Savoir et pouvoir: Philosophie thomiste et politique cléricale aux XIX siècle* (Quebec: Presse de l'Université Laval, 1972).

11. Mannheim, *Ideology and Utopia,* p. 268.

12. In English the term "historicism" is usually associated with a philosophy of total world interpretation. Cf. Karl Popper, *The Poverty of Historicism* (London: Routledge & Kegan Paul, 1957).

13. Cf. Gregory Baum, "Science and Commitment: Historical Truth According to Troeltsch," *Philosophy of the Social Sciences* 1 (1971) pp. 259-77.

14. Mannheim, *Ideology and Utopia,* pp. 78-79, 85-87, 282-84, 305-6.

15. Ibid., pp. 106-7.

16. Ibid., p. 47.

17. Jürgen Habermas' position is discussed in G. Radnitzky, *Continental Schools of Metascience,* pp. 5-8, 147-57.

18. "Declaration on the Question of Admission of Women to the Ministerial Priesthood," Rome, 1976.

19. In German "vulgar Marxism" refers to a reified economic determinism that neglects Marx's dialectical principle. Cf. Georg Lukacs, *History and Class Consciousness* (English trans. of the 1922 German ed.; Cambridge, Mass.: M.I.T. Press, 1971) p. 9.

20. Mannheim, *Ideology and Utopia,* pp. 162-63.

21. Ibid., p. 87.

22. Ibid., pp. 153-64.

23. Ernst Troeltsch, *The Social Teaching of the Christian Churches,* vol. 1 (London: George Allen & Unwin, 1931) p. 331.

24. According to the Third Synod of Bishops, held in Rome in 1971, the church's mission for the redemption of the human race includes "its liberation from every oppressive condition" (*Justice in the World,* Introduction).

25. Mannheim, *Ideology and Utopia,* pp. 279-81.

26. Ibid., p. 88.

The Pere Marquette Theology Lectures

1969: "The Authority for Authority,"
by Quentin Quesnell
Professor of Theology at
Marquette University

1970: "Mystery and Truth,"
by John Macquarrie
Professor of Theology at
Union Theological Seminary, New York

1971: "Doctrinal Pluralism,"
by Bernard Lonergan, S.J.
Professor of Theology at
Regis College, Ontario

1972: "Infallibility,"
by George A. Lindbeck
Professor of Theology at
Yale University

1973: "Ambiguity in Moral Choice,"
by Richard A. McCormick, S.J.
Professor of Moral Theology at
Bellarmine School of Theology

1974: "Church Membership as a Catholic
and Ecumenical Problem,"
by Avery Dulles, S.J.
Professor of Theology at
Woodstock College

1975: "The Contributions of Theology to
Medical Ethics,"
by James Gustafson
University Professor of Theological Ethics at
University of Chicago

1976: "Religious Values in an Age of Violence,"
by Rabbi Marc Tanenbaum
Director of National Interreligious Affairs
American Jewish Committee, New York City

1977: "Truth Beyond Relativism: Karl Mannheim's
Sociology of Knowledge,"
by Gregory Baum
Professor of Theology and Religious Studies at
St. Michael's College

Copies of this lecture and the others in the series are
obtainable from:

Marquette University Press
Marquette University
Milwaukee, Wisconsin 53233
USA

DATE DUE			